Savingforcollege.com

FAMILY GUIDE TO COLLEGE SAVINGS

2014–15 Edition

JOSEPH F. HURLEY, CPA

Savingforcollege.com

Savingforcollege.com's Family Guide to College Savings

Published in the United States by:
Saving For College, LLC
1151 Pittsford-Victor Rd, Ste 103
Pittsford, NY 14534
TELEPHONE: (800) 400–9113
FAX: (585) 286–5428
INTERNET: www.savingforcollege.com
E-MAIL: support@savingforcollege.com

Additional copies of this book may be ordered
directly from the publisher.

Interior design and typesetting by Desktop Miracles, Inc.

Hurley, Joseph F.
Savingforcollege.com's
Family Guide to College Savings

ISBN: 978–0–9815491–6–3

ABOUT THE AUTHOR

Joseph Hurley is founder of Savingforcollege.com, a web-site considered by many to be the best independent source of information on Section 529 state tuition plans and other ways for families to plan and save for college. For over 20 years, he worked as a certified public accountant providing tax-planning services to individuals, business, and tax-exempt organizations.

Hurley is also the author of the first comprehensive book on 529 plans titled *The Best Way To Save For College —A Complete Guide to 529 Plans*. He has been widely quoted in the media, including The Wall Street Journal, TIME, The New York Times, and USA Today and he has appeared at hearings in Washington to present comments on the regulation of 529 plans.

Hurley graduated from Williams College in 1978 and lives with his wife in Victor, New York. They have utilized 529 plans and other education tax benefits in helping to pay the college expenses for their two children.

DISCLAIMER

The information contained in this book and related materials ("Information") is based on information from sources believed to be accurate and reliable and every reasonable effort has been made to make the book and related materials as complete and accurate as possible but such completeness and accuracy cannot be and is not guaranteed. The reader and user of the Information should use this book and related materials as a general guide and not as the ultimate source of information. This book and related materials are not intended to include every possible bit of information regarding the Information but rather to complement and supplement information otherwise available and the reader and user should use the Information accordingly. The Information contains information about tax and other laws and these laws may change. The reader and user should realize that any investment involves risk and the assumptions and projections used in the Information may not be how the investments turn out. The reader and user should consult with their own tax, financial and legal advisors about all of the Information.

THE INFORMATION IS PROVIDED ON AN "AS IS" BASIS WITHOUT ANY WARRANTIES OF ANY KIND, EXPRESS OR IMPLIED. THE AUTHOR, JOSEPH F. HURLEY, THE PUBLISHER, SAVING FOR COLLEGE, LLC, THE DISTRIBUTOR AND ANY OTHER PARTY EXPRESSLY DISCLAIM ANY LIABILITY FOR ANY LOSS OR DAMAGE INCLUDING BUT NOT LIMITED TO ANY LOSS OR DAMAGE FROM ANY USE OF ANY PART OF THE INFORMATION.

IF YOU DO NOT AGREE WITH ANY OF THE TERMS OF THE FOREGOING, YOU SHOULD *NOT* READ THIS BOOK. IF YOU DO NOT RETURN THIS BOOK, YOU WILL BE DEEMED TO HAVE ACCEPTED THE PROVISIONS OF THIS DISCLAIMER.

TABLE OF CONTENTS

INTRODUCTION

Imagine your child coming to you with an acceptance letter from "the" college. The one he's been dreaming of all through high school. The one that perfectly matches her career aspirations. Perhaps even your own alma mater.

Only one thing could make you prouder—knowing that you have done your homework, too. That no matter where your child is accepted or what financial aid is offered, you have the resources to afford the college of choice.

Numerous surveys and studies have been published describing how parents prepare for future college costs. You probably don't need a survey to tell you what you already know:

KIDS GROW TOO FAST.

COLLEGE IS EXPENSIVE.

THE TIME TO START SAVING AND PLANNING IS NOW.

Your child's college tuition could be one of the largest expenditures you ever make. And, if you have more than one child, the financial commitment is compounded. The challenge you face is shared by millions of others.

Fortunately, American families with a desire to save for future college expenses now have more options than ever before. Traditional investment options—savings accounts, taxable investment accounts, annuities, and U.S. Savings Bonds—are joined by more recent investment vehicles including Section 529 college savings programs and Coverdell education savings accounts.

New investment programs bring new opportunities, but they may make decisions more difficult for people who want the best education possible for the children in their lives.

With this *Family Guide to College Savings*, we hope to help you gain a basic understanding of your options so that you can maximize the return on every dollar you set aside for a child's future. Our focus is on the increasingly popular "529 plan," but we also explain other commonly used savings and investment vehicles.

Remember, even if your goal seems overwhelming now, the proper planning and saving can put the cost of any college within your reach.

FEDERAL TAX INCENTIVES TARGETED TO EDUCATION

One of the best ways to increase the affordability of your child's education is to take advantage of federal tax breaks aimed at families saving and paying for college. These include the following:

Qualified Tuition Programs (529 plans)—Earnings grow tax-deferred and distributions are tax-free when used for qualified post-secondary education costs. See page 28 for details.

Coverdell Education Savings Accounts—Earnings grow tax-deferred and distributions are tax-free when used for qualified post-secondary education costs. ESAs can also be withdrawn tax-free for primary and secondary school expenses. See page 43 for details.

U.S. Savings Bonds—EE and I bonds purchased after 1989 by someone at least 24 years old may be redeemed tax-free when bond owners, their spouses, or dependents pay for college tuition and fees. In 2014, the tax exclusion is phased out for incomes between $76,000 and $91,000 (between $113,950 and $143,950 for married taxpayers filing jointly). These income limits increase each year.

Individual Retirement Accounts—Early withdrawal penalties are waived when Roth IRAs and traditional IRAs are used to pay the qualified post-secondary education costs of yourself, your spouse, your children, or your grandchildren. Taxes may still be due on the withdrawals, however.

American Opportunity Tax Credit—Through 2017, a parent can claim a tax credit for 100% of the first $2,000 and 25% of the next $2,000, of a dependent child's college tuition and related expenses (including course materials), for a maximum $2,500 annual tax credit per child. Students can claim the credit only if they are not claimed as a dependent on another person's tax return. The credit is phased out for incomes between $80,000 and $90,000 (between $160,000 and $180,000 for married taxpayers filing jointly). The credit is allowed only for students who are attending a degree program at least half-time and who have not completed their first four years of academic study before the beginning of the taxable year. It cannot not be claimed in more than four tax years for any one student.

For eligible taxpayers—anyone beyond the "kiddie tax" age—as much as 40 percent of the credit is refundable.

Lifetime Learning Credit—A taxpayer may claim a tax credit for 20% of up to $10,000 in combined tuition and mandatory fees for himself, his spouse, and his dependent children. This equates to a $2,000 tax credit. In 2014, the credit is phased out for incomes between $54,000 and $64,000 (between $108,000 and $128,000 for married taxpayers filing jointly). Claiming the American Opportunity credit described above means that you may not claim a Lifetime Learning credit for any of that student's expenses in the same tax year. There is no requirement that the student be studying towards a degree or be enrolled at least half-time, and there is no limit on the number of years the credit may be taken.

Tuition and Fees—An above-the-line deduction (this means you do not have to itemize your deductions) for up to $4,000 of the college tuition and related expenses of yourself, your spouse, or your dependent was available in 2013 for taxpayers with incomes of $65,000 or less ($130,000 or less for married taxpayers filing jointly). For taxpayers with incomes between $65,000 and $80,000 (between $130,000 and $160,000 for married taxpayers filing jointly), the deduction limit was $2,000. The deduction could not be claimed if an American Opportunity or Lifetime Learning credit was claimed. This deduction expired at the end of 2013 and will no longer be available unless Congress restores it.

Deduction for Student-loan Interest—Up to $2,500 in student loan interest may be deducted above-the-line as long as the debt was incurred to pay the college costs for yourself, your spouse, or your dependent, while enrolled as a student at least half-time in a degree program. For 2014, the deduction is phased out for incomes between $65,000 and $80,000 (between $130,000 and $160,000 for married taxpayers filing jointly). A student claimed as a dependent may not take the deduction on his or her own return.

Tax-free Scholarships—Most scholarships and grants are tax-free if the recipient does not have to provide services in exchange for the award.

Tax-free Educational Assistance—Employers may pay and deduct up to $5,250 in college and graduate school costs for each employee under a Section 127 educational assistance plan. The education does not have to be job-related. The benefit is tax-free to the employee, but cannot be used to pay for an employee's children or other family members.

For more information on tax incentives for education, see IRS Publication 970, Tax Benefits for Higher Education, available at www.irs.gov.

YOUR GOAL

Affording the College of Choice

Most people look at the price of a college degree as an expense, like the electric or cable bill. But what if you looked at it as an investment? According to the U.S. Census Bureau, in the year 2009, the average male college graduate, aged 25–34, earned 85% more than the average male who completed only high school or had a General Education Development (GED) certificate. Among women the same age, college graduates earned 111% more than non-graduates.[*]

[*] U.S. Census Bureau, Current Population Survey, 2010 Annual Social and Economic Supplement, based on median earnings.

Over a lifetime, the additional earnings resulting from this "investment" in education could easily exceed $1 million.

Still, the question remains: How will you finance that investment?

Pay as You Go

Your child could help pay for college by getting a job, but students must already juggle studies and other college activities. Even a part-time job might detract from their primary focus—getting an education.

You can also plan to pay college expenses out of your future income as long as you realize that doing so might require substantial cutbacks in other areas of your family budget.

Pay Later

Some might suggest that you approach college tuition as you would buying a home—borrow the money to pay for college and simply repay the debt with higher earnings after graduation. Though many parents see advantages in having children contribute to their education expenses, a college education can be as costly as buying a home. How many parents want their children to start out with such substantial debt?

FIND SOMEONE TO HELP PAY

Scholarships and grants are the ideal financial aid. They don't have to be paid back. But according to the College Board, less than $48 billion of the $170 billion in federal financial aid for the 2012–13 school year came in the form of grants, while over $101 billion was loans. (The rest was federal work-study and the value of education tax benefits.)[*] The states, employers, private organizations, and colleges themselves provided an additional $68 billion in scholarships and grants in 2012–13.

SAVE NOW FOR MORE FREEDOM AND MORE CHOICE LATER

Saving now is the best way to ensure that you have options later. After all, you would like your child to select a college that offers the best education and not necessarily the best financial aid.

You probably also want the comfort of knowing that you won't be dependent on outside sources like loans or scholarships to meet college expenses.

---

[*] The College Board, *Trends in Student Aid 2013.*

Many strategies and investment vehicles are available to help you maximize your college savings. Selecting a suitable strategy and the best combination of investment vehicles is critical. For each option, you face the task of evaluating key characteristics including:

* The potential for growth
* Risk of loss
* Tax implications
* Ownership and control
* Ease of management
* Fees and expenses

The decisions you make now can have a significant impact on how much money is available for tuition payments in the future. In this guide, we focus on the most common components of a sound college savings plan—a plan that can give you and your future college student a high degree of financial security and the confidence that you can afford the college of choice.

THE REAL COST OF HIGHER EDUCATION

An excellent education for your child does not necessarily require that you spend $50,000 in today's dollars for one year's tuition at an Ivy League school. Many non-Ivy private colleges are highly regarded and also reasonably-priced. The average public college or university tuition is lower yet, especially for residents of the state where the school is located.[*]

Type of Institution	Projected 4-Year Tuition and Fees*	
	Today (Enrolling 2014)	In 18 Years (Enrolling 2032)
Private College	$129,700	$312,100
Public University (in-state resident)	$38,300	$92,200
2 Years Community College & 2 Years Private College	$74,700	$179,800

According to The College Board, the average 2013–14 tuition increase was 3.8 percent at private colleges, and 2.9 percent at public universities. The ten-year historical rate of increase has been approximately 5 percent **beyond** the rate of increase in the Consumer Price Index. Average family incomes have not even been close to keeping up.

The figures above do **not** include other costs your child will incur as a college student, such as room and board, books, supplies, equipment, and transportation. These additional expenses can increase your child's cost of attending college by a substantial amount.

---

[*] Based on average published tuition and fees for 2013–14 as reported by The College Board and assumed to increase 5% annually. (The College Board, *Trends in College Pricing 2013*.)

Tough Choices

College Planning Versus Retirement Planning

Paying for college is not your only financial concern. Providing for your own retirement can be even more important since no one offers grants, scholarships, or federally guaranteed loans to support you when you leave the workforce.

Ideally, college and retirement should be part of the same financial plan, but you should still expect some trade-offs as you try to balance these goals. You may have to work longer than you would like or your children may have to borrow more money than they would like. The important thing is that it is possible to meet these two major financial responsibilities.

Keep these key facts in mind when thinking about retirement and college savings:

* Most advisors agree that you should take full advantage of special retirement accounts such as 401(k), IRA, and 403(b) tax-sheltered annuities before funding your college savings accounts. These retirement plans offer special tax advantages, and, in some cases, matching contributions from your employer.

* Assets in retirement accounts will not affect your child's prospects for federal financial aid (unless you actually take distributions from them during the college years). Neither will life insurance or annuities. If your child is earning a small amount from working, a Roth IRA can be a great way to invest unspent income.

* IRAs can even be a secondary source of college funding. Tax law permits you to tap your traditional or Roth IRA for qualified college costs without incurring the 10 percent penalty for distributions before age 59 1/2. Income tax may apply, however.

* Except in unusual circumstances, your 401(k) is less accessible for college. You might be able to borrow from your 401(k), but any money borrowed will have to be paid back in short order.

Just remember that using any of your retirement money to pay for education costs means it won't be there for your own retirement expenses. You probably don't want to support your children through college only to risk becoming a burden to them in your later years.

SPECIAL CONSIDERATIONS FOR GRANDPARENTS

Surveys show that many grandparents want to help fund the college education of their grandchildren, particularly if they already have enough money to ensure a comfortable retirement income. Grandparents in this position should investigate college savings options just as parents do, but often with different objectives in mind.

Typical Grandparent Goals

Concern about the estate planning implications of college savings choices. Many grandparents see a dual benefit in advancing their grandchildren's education and reducing estate tax exposure.

Control and accessibility. You may want to retain control of your funds and keep them easily accessible to you in case of unexpected expenses.

Ease of management. You probably want an investment vehicle that doesn't complicate your overall financial management.

Flexibility. You may have several future college students to think about. They may be spread around the country and their financial situations may vary greatly depending on the financial security of their parents and their other grandparents.

Your Place in the Overall Education Savings Plan

If you decide to assist your grandchildren, it's important to involve their parents in the decision-making process. Your desire to pay college bills directly or to set up educational trusts impacts the financial aid application filed for the student.

And if you gift money or other property to your grandchildren under the Uniform Gifts to Minors Act ("UGMA") or Uniform Transfers to Minors Act ("UTMA"), any future earnings or capital gains will be reported to the child and may require the parents to prepare tax filings.

Be sure to consider the benefits of a 529 plan. Many grandparents find it to be a particularly attractive investment program. Like any other grandparent-owned investment, your 529 plan is not counted as an asset in the determination of financial need for federal student aid programs. However, any money actually spent on behalf of the student must be added to student income on the aid application.

COMPARING COLLEGE SAVINGS ALTERNATIVES

With so many choices available for college savings, you may be unsure about what's right for your family. Selecting the right approach may seem overwhelming. Don't let that stop you from moving forward. Here are the major options, with some of their key advantages and disadvantages to help you with your planning.

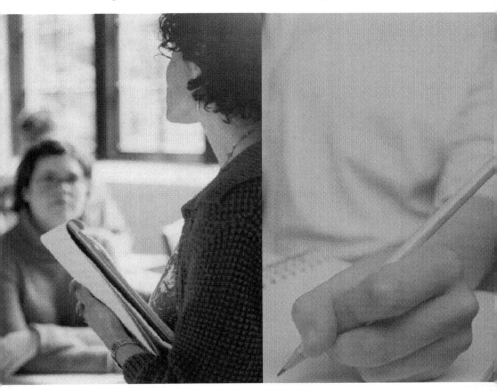

529 PLANS

GENERAL DESCRIPTION

The technical name for 529 plans is "qualified tuition programs" and there are two basic types—the *Section 529 prepaid program and the Section 529 investment program*. Both types provide tax benefits, but they work in different ways. Eleven states currently offer enrollment into a prepaid program, and a group of private colleges has its own prepaid program called the Private College 529 Plan. With the exception of the states of Washington and Wyoming, every state, along with the District of Columbia, offers a 529 investment program. Each 529 plan has certain unique rules and investment characteristics and it's important to find one that suits your specific needs.

In a 529 prepaid program, you make a payment now or a series of payments over time, and the program promises to pay future tuition and fees for a certain number of credit hours or semesters at specified colleges or universities. Though not quite as flexible as 529 investment programs, these plans may be attractive to families seeking a hedge against future tuition increases.

State-run prepaid programs are usually geared to families that intend to send their children to in-state public institutions and may not cover college costs other than tuition and mandatory fees. However, their benefits can always be converted for use at other schools. The conversion method most commonly used is to compute the average in-state tuition and make that amount available for private and out-of-state colleges.

Because you can't be sure your beneficiary will finish college, it is important to understand how much of your "prepaid" money will be refunded if you ever cancel the contract. Some programs will pay interest on your returned payments while others will not. You may also incur cancellation fees.

Section 529 investment programs, which are sometimes referred to as college savings plans ("CSP") or college investment plans ("CIP"), allow you to open an account and make contributions for any individual beneficiary you choose (your child, grandchild, neighbor, or even yourself). Contributions are invested on behalf of your beneficiary, according to the investment strategy you select. All 529 investment programs are state-sponsored and most are open to residents of any state. It generally doesn't matter where your beneficiary attends college. We discuss the 529 investment programs in more detail because they are increasingly popular and provide more choice than the 529 prepaid programs.

How a 529 investment Program Works

Most 529 investment programs offer a menu of investment strategies, including both 1) age-based options
that gradually shift from a concentration in equities to a
concentration in less risky fixed income securities as your
child approaches college age and 2) static options that
maintain a constant blend of equities and fixed income
securities. Often, the underlying investments in these
portfolios are stock and bond mutual funds. Some programs also offer a principal-protected account that earns
a specified level of interest.

Remember, contributions to a 529 investment
program that are invested in stocks and bonds are not
guaranteed to keep up with college inflation. In fact, they
can lose value over any given time period.

When the time comes to withdraw money for
your beneficiary's college costs, you simply direct the
529 program administrator to send a distribution from
your account either to you or to your beneficiary. Most
programs will even pay college bills directly upon
your instruction. Distributions can be taken for any
purpose; however, distributions during any year that
total up to more than the qualifying college expenses
incurred during that year can result in income taxes
and penalties.

CORE BENEFITS OF A 529 INVESTMENT PROGRAM

✳ **Professional investment management.** Most states have hired outside investment firms or mutual fund companies to design and manage their 529 investment programs.

✳ **Flexibility.** You may change the beneficiary on the account to another qualifying family member at any time. In addition, your 529 account can be rolled over to a different state's 529 plan without triggering federal taxes provided no other rollover for your beneficiary has occurred within the prior twelve months.

✳ **Generous contribution limits.** Low minimum contribution requirements and high maximum contribution limits generally let families invest as little or as much as they can afford. Federal law imposes no annual contribution limits on 529 plans and many 529 investment programs have lifetime contribution limits exceeding $300,000 per beneficiary. Minimum contributions are typically low, usually under $100, and many 529 investment programs allow systematic investments through automatic withdrawals from your bank account or deductions from your paycheck.

✳ **Control.** You maintain ownership and control of the 529 account. You make all decisions including when to withdraw money and what to use it for. You can even take it back for yourself. Your beneficiary generally has no rights to the account no matter how old she is.

Tax Advantages of a 529 Plan

Federal income tax

The most attractive benefit of a 529 investment or pre-paid program is that all money contributed to the plan can grow tax-deferred and be withdrawn tax-free for qualified college costs. Although contributions are not deductible on your federal income tax return, the tax-deferred compounding of any earnings can be a powerful factor in eventually meeting tuition expenses.

Here's how the tax advantage works:

＊ You select a 529 plan and make your contribution(s). You then receive periodic statements (annual, quarterly, or monthly) for each account you own. However, even as your account grows, there is nothing to report on your income tax return, unless you take a distribution. You will probably take distributions once your beneficiary enters college.

＊ Once distributions begin, you or your beneficiary (depending on program procedures) will receive a Form 1099-Q from the program administrator reporting any distributions during the year. This form specifies the principal and earnings portions of the distribution (computed pro-rata).

✳ In preparing your or your beneficiary's income tax return, count up the qualified higher education expenses incurred during the year. If these are greater than the amount of distributions, no taxes are owed. If they are less, some portion of the earnings is taxed as ordinary income and is also subject to an additional 10 percent penalty tax.

Qualified higher education expenses currently include tuition, fees, books, supplies, and equipment expenses required for full-time or part-time attendance at an eligible educational institution, plus the special needs expenses of special needs beneficiaries. Room and board is considered a qualified expense as long as the student is attending a degree program on at least a half-time basis. Just about any accredited college or graduate school is an eligible institution, including many vocational and professional schools. Foreign schools are also eligible if their students can participate in federal financial aid programs.

State income tax

If your state imposes an income tax, it is likely to follow the federal tax treatment of your 529 plan, whether or not you choose the plan from that state. However, you should always be certain you understand the tax rules in your own state. (If you decide to open an account in a different state, you shouldn't have to worry about paying taxes to that other state unless you or your beneficiary subsequently becomes a resident.)

Thirty-three states and the District of Columbia currently offer their residents a state tax deduction or tax credit for contributions to their 529 plans. If your state is one of them, you should consider the value of that deduction when deciding whether or not to open an account in your state's plan. Most states place an annual limit on the amount of the deduction, although a few do not. Currently, if you live in Arizona, Kansas, Maine, Missouri, Montana, or Pennsylvania, you can receive a state tax deduction for contributions you make to 529 plans outside your home state.

Estate and gift tax

Another benefit of 529 plans is their usefulness in estate planning. The value of your 529 account is not included in your gross estate. Individuals with sizable estates typically find this benefit very attractive.

However, contributions to a 529 plan are treated as a gift from you to the named beneficiary on the account. If the beneficiary is a grandchild, you may also be subject to the generation-skipping transfer ("GST") tax.

Even considering the gift tax, 529 plans are attractive. In 2014, you can use your $14,000 ($28,000 for a married couple) per-donee annual exclusion to avoid gift tax and GST tax.* Any contributions larger than your available annual exclusion must be reported on a gift tax return and will consume part of your $5.34 million (in 2014) lifetime gift exemption.

You can also take advantage of a special five-year election that allows you to put as much as $70,000 into a 529 plan for each child immediately without gift tax or GST tax. This uses up all or part of your annual exclusions for the next five years.

Gift tax issues can also occur later in the life of a 529 account. There is no gift tax consequence if you change the beneficiary of the account to another family member in the same generation, such as a sibling or cousin. However, if you change the beneficiary to another family member who is at least one generation below the former beneficiary, the former beneficiary may be required to treat the value of the account as a gift to the new beneficiary. Be sure to review any gift tax consequences before changing beneficiaries.

---

* Be sure to count other cash or property gifts you make to your beneficiary during the year in determining how much of this exclusion is still available for your 529 plan contributions.

POSSIBLE DISADVANTAGES TO A 529 PLAN

✳ **Penalties for non-qualified distributions.** If distributions exceed qualifying college education costs, you will owe ordinary income tax and a 10 percent penalty on earnings. The resulting tax bill may be much higher than the taxes on an alternative investment (like an UGMA/UTMA investment account) that qualifies for capital gains treatment. The 10 percent penalty is waived if the distribution is attributable to the beneficiary's death, disability, receipt of a scholarship, or claiming the American Opportunity or Lifetime Learning credit. One way to avoid taxes and penalties when the original beneficiary doesn't need the money for school is to change the beneficiary to another qualifying family member.

✳ **Program costs.** In addition to the cost of underlying mutual funds, most 529 plans charge a modest investment or program management fee against the value of your account. There may also be an enrollment fee, annual account maintenance, rollover fees, and other transaction expenses. If you open an account through a financial advisor, you may incur a sales charge or additional annual expenses that compensate advisors for their services. Fees and expenses are disclosed in the program enrollment materials.

✳ **Gift taxes.** There are ways to pay for college that do not involve gift taxes. Under most state statutes, parents can simply pay their child's college costs as part of their overall support. Similarly, grandparents or other relatives can pay tuition directly to the school without gift-tax consequences.

✳ **Regulations and restrictions.** Owners have little or no control over how a state operates its 529 plan. Program rules and fees can be changed at any time. The state can also change the investments (or the investment manager) under certain conditions. If you don't like the changes being made, your only recourse is to request a non-qualified distribution or roll over your account to another 529 plan.

✳ **Investment changes.** You may switch among your plan's investment options whenever you change beneficiaries on the account. However, the IRS has placed a limit of one switch per calendar year if the beneficiary is not changed.

CHOOSING A 529 PLAN

Start by investigating the 529 plans offered by your own state and by the state where your beneficiary resides. You may discover that there are benefits for residents that are not available to you by participating in a different state's 529 plan. For example:

* Find out if your state offers a state income tax deduction or tax credit for some or all contributions to its 529 plan.

* A few states offer a partial match of contributions for low-income families or a scholarship for beneficiaries. Or they may give their residents a break on program expenses and fees.

* A state may exclude the value of your account when determining eligibility for state-funded financial aid programs.

* Creditor protection and other legal concerns may be more clearly defined with your own state's 529 plan.

* Residents of Alabama must use the in-state 529 plan in order to avoid paying state income tax on qualified distributions. Residents of other states do not face this restriction.

Once you've considered your own state's plan, take a look at what other states offer. Despite the potential advantages of a same-state investment, thousands of investors are choosing other states' 529 plans. The attraction of an out-of-state plan may include the quality of the investment options or the regulations of the program. You may even decide to establish accounts in more than one 529 plan in order to meet all your objectives.

When choosing a 529 plan be sure to evaluate the following factors:

Investment Options. Make sure your 529 plan offers at least one option that meets your investment objectives and tolerance for risk. Consider stocks, bonds, and interest-bearing accounts with principal protection, as well as a blend of these. Some 529 plans offer mutual funds from a single fund family while others select mutual funds from a number of different fund families. Decide which approach seems better for you. Ask about special investment features, like a program that matches your investment to your child's age, automatically shifting away from stocks and toward fixed income investments as college approaches.

You will probably want to consider the performance of the investment portfolios available through the plan; however it's not a good idea to select a 529 plan based strictly on historical investment performance. Many 529 savings programs have not been around long enough to have meaningful track records. Even if they were, it is sometimes difficult to make an "apples to apples" comparison when their investment portfolios have different stock and bond allocation targets. To get some idea of how the investments in a particular 529 plan have performed, look for the results in official program disclosures. You may also be able to research the investment performance and characteristics of the underlying mutual funds by accessing individual fund company Web sites.

Expenses. Be sure you understand all program fees and investment expenses as well as the impact they will have on your overall return. Some 529 savings programs will "wrap" the underlying mutual fund expenses into their program management fees while others will keep them separate.

Professional Assistance. Developing a financial plan for college, researching the investment options, and making appropriate decisions can take substantial time and effort. If you are comfortable doing this on your own, you may be able to reduce your costs with "direct-sold" 529 plans. On the other hand, if you want the assistance of a financial advisor, you can work with a fee-based financial planner or a commission-based broker. Several 529 plans are sold only through financial professionals.

Program Structure and Restrictions. Because 529 savings plans are custom-crafted by individual states, rules and restrictions vary from plan to plan. Review the overall plan structure. Some differences are obvious, such as maximum and minimum contribution levels. Other factors may be more difficult to discern but could be even more important for 529 owners and beneficiaries:

✳ Will you be allowed to transfer the ownership of your account to another individual, or to a trust?

* Who ends up controlling the account if you die? Are you permitted to designate a successor owner on the application? And what happens if you don't designate one?

* How quickly will your contributions be invested after being received by the program administrator, and how long will it take for your withdrawal requests to be processed?

* Do you have to use the account within a specified number of years, or by the time your beneficiary reaches a specified age?

* What are the withdrawal procedures? Does the 529 plan provide you with the ability to the select either the account owner, beneficiary, or school as recipient in all instances?

In general, you want a 529 plan that takes advantage of all the power and flexibility permitted under federal tax law. If the plan that best suits your needs doesn't offer every feature you want, you can open accounts in more than one program or roll over your account to another plan before a restriction becomes a problem.

THE RESIDENCY FACTOR

To enroll in a 529 plan, most programs require only that you be at least 18 years old and that both you and your beneficiary have a valid Social Security number or taxpayer identification number. Although some 529 investment programs and nearly all prepaid programs require that you or your beneficiary reside or work for an employer within the sponsoring state, many 529 plans have no state residency restrictions.

Increasingly, states are offering one version of their 529 investment programs to state residents, and another version to others, including nonresidents and residents who open their account through a broker or a partici-pating employer. The two versions may have different expenses and may even offer different investment options.

For further information and links to all the 529 plans, visit the following Web sites:

✳ The Internet Guide to 529 Plans at www.savingforcollege.com

✳ College Savings Plan Network at www.collegesavings.org

COVERDELL EDUCATION SAVINGS ACCOUNT

GENERAL DESCRIPTION

A Coverdell education savings account (sometimes known as a "Coverdell account", "ESA", or "CESA") lets parents, grandparents, other family members, friends or even the child contribute money to a tax-advantaged account for future education expenses. Individuals making contributions to Coverdell ESAs must meet certain income requirements described below.

To open an ESA, you may contact an investment broker or any financial institution that offers the type of investment (stocks, bonds, mutual funds, certificates of deposit, etc.) you wish to hold in the account.

You will sign an agreement that names a beneficiary and a "responsible individual" and indicates whether the beneficiary assumes control at the age of 18 or the control stays with the responsible individual. Most ESA agreements require that the responsible individual be the beneficiary's parent or guardian. This can make the ESA less attractive for grandparents or other relatives.

※ The beneficiary of the ESA must be under 18 years old when each contribution is made. Beneficiaries with "special needs" may be older than 18.

* Combined contributions on behalf of any one child may not exceed the annual contribution limit of $2,000. Contributions in excess of limit incur a federal excise tax. You have until April 15 of next year to make this year's contribution.

* The contributor must have income less than $95,000 ($190,000 if married and filing a joint tax return) in order to make the maximum $2,000 contribution. A partial contribution is allowed for incomes up to $110,000 ($220,000 joint). If your income is too high, another adult or even your child may make the contribution with their own money.

TAX ADVANTAGES OF A COVERDELL ESA

Like a 529 plan, earnings in an ESA are tax-deferred and can be withdrawn free of federal taxes in a year during which the beneficiary incurs qualified education expenses.

CORE BENEFITS OF A COVERDELL ESA

For some families, an ESA may make more sense than a 529 plan for the first dollars being committed to college savings each year. Here are the reasons why:

✳ **Wide range of available investments.** An ESA can include most types of investments, including stocks, bonds, fixed rate accounts, and all types of mutual funds. Since most financial institutions offer ESAs you can choose any investment or mix of investments that suits your situation. You can change investments within the account as often as you desire. You can also roll over some or all of your account to another ESA as often as once every twelve months.

✳ **Broad definition of education expenses.** Unlike 529 plans, which may only be used for higher education expenses, an ESA can be withdrawn tax-free to pay for elementary and secondary school costs as well as certain college expenses. Private school tuition and many other costs at both private and public schools for grades K — 12 are eligible, including transportation, uniforms, and supplies. You can even withdraw money tax-free from an ESA to pay for a home computer or Internet access.

✳ **Simplicity.** Because the ESA was created by the federal government, it is a simpler and more uniform investment vehicle than the state-sponsored 529 plans. Like the IRA, every provider of ESAs follows the same basic model, making the actual investment options the primary factor in your selection.

Possible disadvantages to a Coverdell ESA

✳ ESAs are less appropriate for older students since the money must be distributed by age 30. Special-needs beneficiaries are exempted from this requirement.

✳ While the responsible individual listed on the account may direct the investment of ESA funds and maintain control over the timing and use of withdrawals, the money set aside in an ESA must be for the exclusive benefit of the named beneficiary. In this aspect, it is similar to a UGMA or UTMA account, except that you may be able to keep any excess funds out of the beneficiary's hands until age 30.

✳ At age 30 the account must terminate. Any remaining assets are paid to the beneficiary subject to income tax and a 10 percent penalty on the earnings. You can set up the ESA so that you have the right to change the beneficiary to another family member who is under the age of 30.

✳ Given the relatively low $2,000 annual contribution limit, maintenance fees as a percentage of your account may be higher than on vehicles that permit larger investments.

✳ Contributions to an ESA are potentially subject to gift tax just like a 529 plan.

UGMA/UTMA ACCOUNTS

GENERAL DESCRIPTION

UGMA/UTMA accounts are investments owned by your child. Because minors are not permitted by law to handle investments directly, the account is placed under the control of a custodian (in most cases the parent) subject to the state's Uniform Gifts to Minors Act ("UGMA") or the more recently adopted Uniform Transfers to Minors Act ("UTMA"). A custodial account is easy to establish at any financial institution and can hold most types of financial assets including stocks, bonds, fixed-rate accounts and mutual funds.

Often, UGMA/UTMA accounts are used to invest money given to a child from grandparents or other relatives and family friends. Grandparents may make these gifts to reduce estate taxes, although the gift tax and generation-skipping transfer tax must be considered. (For large amounts a formal trust may be preferable to UGMA/UTMA accounts.)

TAX ADVANTAGES OF UGMA/UTMA ACCOUNTS

UGMA/UTMA accounts also offer parents the opportunity to reduce income taxes by shifting investment income from a high income tax bracket to a child's lower bracket. This would produce higher after-tax returns, providing more money for college. This strategy works best with older children. Before the year in which the child turns 18, only $2,000 (in 2014) in annual investment income is taxed at the child's rate; investment earnings above that amount are taxed at the parent's marginal rate. This is the so-called "kiddie tax."

Beginning in 2008, the kiddie tax was expanded to include 18-year olds as well as to include full-time college students ages 19 through 23 who do not provide over one-half of their support through their own wage and self-employment earnings. This change undoubtedly places an added financial burden on many families at the time they need the money most—to pay college bills.

Possible Disadvantages to UGMA/UTMA Accounts

✳ **Loss of control to child.** The biggest deterrent to keeping large amounts in an UGMA/UTMA account is probably the prospect of your child obtaining direct ownership and control of any unspent funds at a certain age (either 18 or 21, depending on state law). Even before reaching this magic age your child may view the account as a future party fund rather than a college fund. A small account may not be a concern because you can probably spend the account on education or in other ways that benefit your child before he or she takes direct control.

✳ **Added tax paperwork.** Form 1040 must be filed for any year in which a dependent child's investment income exceeds the standard deduction ($1,000 in 2014). Preparing a child's income tax return and paying quarterly estimated taxes can be an added headache for parents.

✳ **Impact on financial aid.** Student-owned investments including UGMA/UTMA accounts are counted heavily in the determination of financial need. The income tax savings of shifting income to the lower tax bracket can backfire if the money reduces the financial aid package. For more information, see the discussion in "Financial Aid Considerations" on page 62.

TAXABLE INVESTMENT ACCOUNTS

GENERAL DESCRIPTION

Education savings can be invested in a regular taxable mutual fund or brokerage account. This provides a wide range of investment options and the ability to design an investment portfolio that suits your specific needs.

There are other advantages as well. You can avoid some of the drawbacks of placing investment funds in an UGMA/UTMA account while your child is young by keeping certain stocks and stock mutual funds in your own name. You can then transfer them to your child shortly before they are needed to pay for college costs. Any capital gains generated by the sale of the investments are reported on your child's tax return, providing tax savings up to the kiddie tax threshold.

This approach can also produce a better financial aid package by letting you time the transfer and sale of appreciated investments to minimize the amount of your "expected family contribution" to college costs.

Tax Implications of Taxable Investment Accounts

Income Taxes

Maintaining a taxable investment account (in your name or the child's) may not work as well as tax-free 529 plans or ESAs, especially if you invest in income-generating assets such as bonds and bank certificates of deposit, or if your stock portfolio generates significant annual dividends or capital gains. Consider keeping the more income-oriented portion of your investments in 529 plans and ESAs even if you plan to hold equities in your taxable investment account.

One advantage a taxable investment account has over a 529 or ESA is that you may pay lower capital gains tax rates, even if you do not use the money for "qualified" purposes. Remember, earnings in a 529 or ESA that are distributed for purposes other than qualified education expenses are subject to tax at ordinary income rates plus a 10 percent penalty rate.

Gift Taxes

Federal gift taxes are another issue to consider when holding appreciated stocks or mutual funds in a taxable account and then transferring them into a child's UGMA/UTMA account just before college. If you transfer property to your child, even if it is later used for college expenses, the value of the property that does not fall within your $14,000 (in 2014) annual gift tax exclusion will have to be reported as a taxable gift on a federal gift tax form. The alternative is to liquidate your stocks or mutual funds and pay the college expenses yourself, without gift tax consequences in most situations. Grandparents may be especially interested in the unlimited gift exclusion for direct payment of tuition to an educational institution. But the capital gains from selling your investments will now be reported on your own tax return.

Transferring Assets
Between Accounts

Many families may already have money in one type of college savings vehicle and now want to move it to another type. This is certainly possible, but it is important to look at all aspects of the transfer, including ownership considerations, income tax implications and gift tax consequences. Here we review some of the most common transfers.

UGMA/UTMA TO 529 PLAN

The income tax advantages and investment approaches offered in a 529 plan may make them a more attractive choice for your child's UGMA/UTMA money. Most 529 plans accept money from UGMAs and UTMAs, either by permitting the custodian to establish the account, or by providing a checkbox on the 529 application to indicate that an UGMA/UTMA is the source of contributed funds. A few 529 plans are less accommodating and leave it to you (and your legal and tax and financial advisors) to figure out how the transfer can be accomplished under relevant state law.

In any event, if the money in a 529 account came from an UGMA/UTMA:

* The beneficiary of the account can no longer be changed

* Any distributions must be for the benefit of the child, and

* When the child reaches the age of 18 or 21 (depending on the particular state law), the custodianship terminates and the child becomes the direct owner of the 529 account

It's important to put non-UGMA/UTMA money into a separate 529 account so that you can retain control and ownership. In fact, rather than transferring UGMA/ UTMA money to a 529 plan, you may even want to use that money for discretionary expenditures before the child reaches the age of majority—for example summer camp expenses—and replace it with new money put into your self-owned 529 account.

Finally, 529 plans can only accept cash, so a transfer of appreciated securities from an UGMA/UTMA account requires liquidation of those securities, possibly triggering capital gains.

UGMA/UTMA to ESA

Transferring money from an UGMA/UTMA account to a Coverdell education savings account (ESA) appears straightforward—both types of account are held by a custodian for the benefit of the child. However, such a transfer may prevent any future beneficiary changes and may require turning over control of the ESA to the child at the age of 18. You should seek legal guidance if you have concerns about this. Like the 529 plan, ESAs only accept cash so the liquidation of appreciated securities in order to transfer money from an UGMA/UTMA account can create a tax liability.

ESA to 529 Plan

If your child has an ESA, money from that account can be transferred to a 529 account without triggering a tax liability, as long as that child remains the beneficiary of the 529 account. This could be an effective strategy if your child is about to turn age 30 with unspent funds in an ESA.

This does not work in reverse; transfers from a 529 account to an ESA are treated as distributions subject to tax and penalty.

In any tax-free transfer from an ESA to a 529 account, the untaxed earnings in the ESA must be reported to the 529 plan so that a "basis" adjustment can be made. This ensures that those earnings are reported as taxable income in the event that any future distributions from the 529 plan are non-qualified distributions.

There are no clear regulations regarding the ownership rights in a 529 account that receives money from an ESA. However, similar to the UGMA/UTMA accounts, certain restrictions may be necessary to preserve the legal rights of the ESA beneficiary.

529 to 529

You can transfer all or a portion of one 529 account to another 529 account by using a rollover. Rollovers cannot be performed more than once in a 12-month period if you wish to keep the same beneficiary on the new account. Rollovers to an account with a different family member as beneficiary can be performed as often as you want.

There are two ways to roll over funds between 529 plans. The first is to make a contribution to a new 529 plan within 60 days after withdrawing funds from your current 529 account. The second is to request a direct "trustee-to-trustee" transfer. Either way, the tax basis of the rolled over funds must be reported to your new 529 plan so that the untaxed earnings remain accounted for. Be sure to consider other effects of a rollover, including transaction fees, gift taxes and the possible recapture of state income tax deductions claimed on the original contributions.

ESA TO ESA

You may roll over money that is withdrawn from an ESA into another ESA for the same beneficiary or for a member of the beneficiary's family who is under age 30. The money must be deposited into the new account within 60 days of the withdrawal and can be done only once in a 12-month period. The law is not clear on whether a direct "trustee-to-trustee" transfer of ESA funds is subject to the 12-month requirement so check with your tax advisor first.

U.S. SAVINGS BONDS TO 529 OR ESA

Qualified Series EE bonds or I Bonds may be redeemed free of tax if the redemption proceeds are placed into a 529 account that names yourself, your spouse or your child as beneficiary. If the 529 account names your child, you must be able to claim that child as a dependent on your income tax return. Therefore, grandparents owning qualified savings bonds generally can't make this tax-free transfer.

Savings bond proceeds can also be transferred tax-free to an ESA for your dependent child. However, the low per-child annual cap on ESA contributions limits the usefulness of the technique.

To be "qualified", savings bonds must have been issued after 1989 and you must have been at least 24 years old at the date of issuance. In order to receive the full tax exclusion, your income must also be less than $76,000 if you redeem the bonds in 2014 ($113,950 if you file a joint tax return).

If you are satisfied with your investment in U.S. Savings Bonds, you might want to wait to redeem the bonds in a year when you, your spouse, or your dependent child is in college. As long as tuition and fees are equal to or greater than the redemption proceeds of your qualified savings bonds and your income is below the phase-out levels in that year, your redemption proceeds will be tax-free.

It may be wise to convert the qualified savings bonds to a 529 savings plan or Coverdell education savings account if your income currently falls below the income limits for tax-free redemption, but you expect it to exceed that threshold during the future college years. This way you lock in the tax benefit on the accrued bond interest.

IRA OR 401(K) TO 529 OR ESA

You cannot transfer money from an IRA, Roth IRA or 401(k) into a 529 account or ESA. Any such transfer would be treated as a distribution from the qualified retirement account subject to all the usual tax rules (including possible penalties).

FINANCIAL AID
CONSIDERATIONS

Seventy-one percent of all college undergraduates received some type of financial aid during the 2011–2012 school year, so it makes sense to explore this avenue for your own child.* Most financial aid is provided by the federal and state governments. Colleges, scholarship organizations, and employers are also important aid sources.

Financial aid can include "self-help"—interest-subsidized loans and work-study—and "gift aid" consisting of grants and scholarships. Gift aid is more attractive, of course, because it doesn't have to be paid back and doesn't place additional demands on the child.

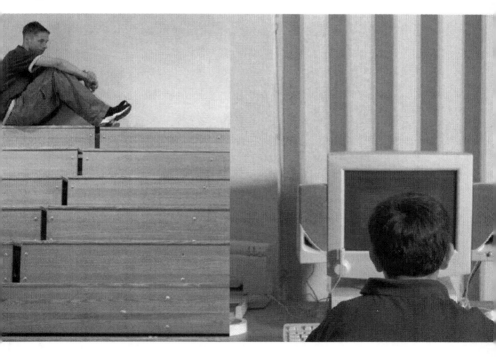

---

* Source: National Center for Education Statistics National Postsecondary Student Aid Study: Undergraduate Financial Aid Estimates by Type of Institution in 2011–12

The amount and type of financial aid offered is based on two factors: the student's merit (scholastic, athletic, musical, etc.) and the student's financial need. Here, we focus on financial need since that is the factor most impacted by your investment decisions.

Three basic ingredients determine how much need-based aid your child is eligible for.

1 **The cost of the school your child is considering or already attending.** Every school calculates its "cost of attendance" or "COA" based on federal guidelines. As you might expect, many private colleges have a high COA while public universities and colleges have a relatively low COA for state residents.

2 **The dollar amount of "resources" provided to the student from outside sources.** Scholarships, for example, are considered a resource. So are payments of tuition directly to the college by a grandparent or employer. A resource will reduce the COA, and therefore the need-based aid award, on a dollar-for-dollar basis.

3 **The "expected family contribution" or "EFC."** This is the amount your family will be expected to pay for college based on your particular financial circumstances. This figure is determined

each school year by the federal government with data you provide on the Free Application for Federal Student Aid (FAFSA). The calculation considers the student's income and assets and the parent's income and assets. (For independent students, parental income and assets are excluded.) The parents' contribution is divided by the number of family members attending college at least half-time.

Assume, for example, that your child is planning to attend a private college costing $25,000 per year. Your expected family contribution is $15,000, consisting of the student's contribution of $2,000 and your contribution of $13,000. A local civic organization has awarded your child a $1,000 scholarship. Your child's financial need is determined to be $9,000 computed as follows:

1 Cost of attendance   **$25,000**

2 Expected family contribution

   Student's contribution   **$ 2,000**

   Parents' contribution   **$13,000**

   Total family contribution   **$15,000**

3 Resources   **$ 1,000**

4 Financial need = (1)−(2)−(3)   **$ 9,000**

The school will attempt to put together an aid package that covers the $9,000 in need. This package can be a combination of grants, loans, and work-study from federal, state, and college sources.

FINANCIAL AID AND YOUR SAVINGS

In order to determine the investment mix that offers the most favorable impact on your child's federal financial aid eligibility, let's first look at how the formula for computing EFC works. The formula counts the following financial resources as being available to pay college expenses:

* 20% of a student's assets (money, investments, business interests, and real estate)

* 50% of a student's income (after certain allowances)

* 2.6%–5.6% of a parent's assets (money, investments, certain business interests, and real estate, based on a sliding income scale and after certain allowances)

* 22%–47% of a parent's income (based on a sliding income scale and after certain allowances)

Now let's see how specific types of assets affect the aid formula:

* A favorable asset to own when applying for financial aid is a retirement account such as an

IRA or 401(k). These qualified retirement accounts, whether owned by you or by your child, are not counted at all in determining EFC for purposes of federal financial aid. Be careful, however, about taking money out of your IRA (or any retirement account) to pay for college. Though the tax law now permits penalty-free withdrawals from a traditional or Roth IRA to pay for qualified college costs, doing so could jeopardize financial aid in the following year. The entire withdrawal, principal and earnings, counts as income on the following year's aid application.

The equity in your primary home, a family-owned business, insurance policies, and annuities are also excluded from your assets when determining EFC.

∗ Assets that belong to the student result in a greater reduction in financial aid. UGMA/UTMA accounts are counted as the student's assets. In addition, they may increase the student's included income to the extent that interest, dividends, or capital gains are reported on the student's income tax return. Often the income tax benefit of setting aside investment assets in a child's name is more or less offset by the reduction in the child's financial aid package.

∗ 529 plans and Coverdell ESAs may be two of the better options to save for college without jeopardizing financial aid. Congress has bestowed these investments with special advantages for aid-eligibility purposes.

If a parent owns the 529 account or ESA, up to 5.6% of the value is included in EFC as a parent asset. If grandparents own the account, none of the value is included.

A 529 account or ESA owned by a dependent student, or by a custodian for the student, does not have to be included with other student-owned investments. Starting with the 2009–10 school year, such accounts are to be reported on the federal aid application (FAFSA) as parental assets.

Withdrawals from 529 plans and ESAs are also treated advantageously. Such withdrawals when used for college are excluded from your federal income tax return, and except for withdrawals from a 529 plan owned by a grandparent or other third party are not required to be "added back" when reporting income on the FAFSA.

✳ Note that some colleges will calculate financial need using a different formula when offering their own grants and tuition discounts. The "institutional methodology" used by many of these colleges may count home equity, siblings' assets, and certain investment accounts in a manner that differs from the federal methodology.

By now you're probably thinking that the financial-aid system is as complicated as the federal income tax, and that might be right. The summary presented here only scratches the surface. Navigating these murky waters may seem difficult, but remember these four basic points:

1 No matter what the rules say, college financial aid officers have great latitude in determining the aid package your child ultimately receives. Officers sometimes use "professional judgment" to adjust the figures—increasing the amount of aid or creating a more attractive ratio between gift aid and self-help aid. They might be more apt to do so if they see other reasons to want your child, such as special abilities or unique characteristics.

2 The rules are constantly changing. The way the financial aid system works today may not be the way it works when your child is ready for college.

3 Your investment decisions now do not necessarily lock you in for purposes of future financial aid eligibility. You will likely have many additional opportunities to enhance your child's prospects for aid.

4 Saving for college reduces your reliance on an uncertain financial aid system. Some families make the mistake of spending because they believe that saving puts them in a worse position to receive financial aid. Planning and saving for college helps you control your family's destiny no matter what the future brings.

OTHER LEGAL ISSUES

You may have additional questions about the impact of college savings on your overall financial situation. For example, what happens to your college savings account if you die? What happens if you are sued or file bankruptcy? Will it affect your application for Medicaid assistance if you enter a nursing home?

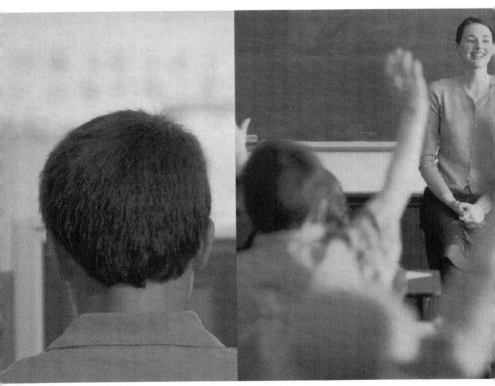

An attorney experienced in these matters is the best person to guide you as you consider the possibility of future events that might derail your best-laid plans for college. The laws of your own state, along with the state of any other party seeking an interest in your property, will usually control the outcome when there is a dispute or action.

529 Plans

Because 529 plans are somewhat new, they are also relatively untested in some of the areas described above. The fact that the account owner generally has unrestricted access to the funds in a 529 account may make it more vulnerable to creditors than money in a qualified retirement plan, IRA, or well-drafted trust. It also may mean that state Medicaid agencies are likely to consider 529 accounts as a source of payment for medical and nursing home bills before Medicaid assistance is made available.

Several states provide their 529 plans with statutory protection from creditor's claims. How this protection extends to plan participants in other states remains uncertain. Beginning in 2005, 529 accounts under certain conditions gain added protections under the federal bankruptcy law.

COVERDELL EDUCATION SAVINGS ACCOUNTS

An ESA is generally less accessible to creditors. These accounts are established for the benefit of the child and do not provide you or other contributors with rights of ownership. Many states have extended their protections for qualified retirement plans and IRAs to ESAs as well, and the 2005 bankruptcy protection changes also apply to ESAs.

PROTECTING COLLEGE SAVINGS THROUGH AN IRREVOCABLE TRUST

Irrevocable trusts are another option for the protection-minded investor. Your attorney can help you establish and fund a trust with spendthrift provisions to ensure use of the assets for the purposes you deem important. Trusts can be expensive to set up and maintain, however, so you would need to have sufficient assets to justify that cost. You will also need to plan for the payment of income tax on earnings generated by taxable investments held in the trust. The income tax bracket for a trust that does not distribute all its income each year becomes very high very quickly.

Putting Your Plan Together

You probably already realize that there are too many pieces in the college savings puzzle for us to offer a plan that fits every family. Your particular circumstances determine what's best for you. However, we can offer some general advice that may help you.

Establish a savings budget. One of the first steps you should take in planning for your child's future college expenses is to establish a savings goal. There are many very useful college cost calculators on the Internet and we encourage you to utilize them. But you can also get a rough idea of how much you should be saving every month just by referring to the chart below. It shows the monthly savings goal from now through college graduation for a family with one child expected to enroll in the average four-year public university, the average four-year private college, or the average Ivy League college/university.

You can easily adjust these targets based on (1) the current four-year cost of the college or university your child expects to enroll in, and (2) the amount of savings you already have set aside for college. Simply compute the difference between those two figures (your "savings gap") and estimate a result using the table.

Monthly Savings Goal Through Final Month of College*			
Type of school		Public	Private
Current annual costs**		$22,826	$44,750
Child's Age	Newborn	$512	$1,003
	Four	$599	$1,175
	Eight	$740	$1,450
	Twelve	$1,004	$1,968
	Sixteen	$1,690	$3,313

* Assumes 5% annual college cost increase and 6% annual investment return.

** Current annual costs are based on The College Board, *Trends in Student Pricing 2013*.

Minimize taxes. Take advantage of the fact that your child can receive up to $1,000 in investment income without paying federal income tax (and at low tax rates above that amount as long as the kiddie tax doesn't apply). By gifting income-generating assets into a UTMA account now, or gifting appreciated assets later, you can effectively shift income and capital gains out of your higher tax bracket. The opportunities for tax savings may be even better if you can employ your child in the family business. Remember that any assets gifted to your children are theirs to control when they reach a certain age under state law, and that a student's assets and income are counted more heavily under financial aid formulas. Be sure to speak with your tax advisor before making any tax-related decisions.

Consider 529 investment programs and Coverdell accounts even for older children. Just because your child is already in high school doesn't mean you can't benefit from tax-advantaged college plans. If your most recent Form 1040 shows income tax on interest, dividends, or capital gains distributions, you have the chance to save taxes with a 529 plan or ESA even if only for a few years. If your state offers a tax deduction for contributions to its 529 plan, you might even benefit by opening an account and soon thereafter start taking distributions to pay college bills.

Invest tax-free whenever possible. If your child will be attending a private or religious elementary or secondary school, consider opening an ESA. If your child still has money in the ESA after high school it can then be used tax-free for college.

Create the right asset mix between your taxable and tax-free investments. If you maintain a fully taxable investment portfolio and a 529 plan or ESA, consider concentrating the growth portion of your investments in the taxable accounts and the income-producing portion in your 529 account or ESA. Growth stocks and low-turnover equity mutual funds are already tax-efficient and can take advantage of low capital gains rates, while income-producing investments are less tax-efficient and can benefit from the tax shelter of a 529 plan or ESA. Capital losses in a taxable investment can also provide a tax benefit, while a 529 plan or ESA cannot produce a capital loss.[*]

Put the right person in control. Grandparents using a 529 plan to save for a grandchild's college education should open the account in their names if they want to maintain

---

[*] A taxpayer liquidating a 529 account at a loss may be able to claim a miscellaneous itemized deduction. The deduction will only provide a tax benefit if the taxpayer itemizes deductions, has total miscellaneous itemized deductions in excess of 2%-of-adjusted gross income, and is not subject to the alternative minimum tax.

control and retain the ability to change the beneficiary to another grandchild. However, if the grandparents prefer that the parent control the account, they can simply make a contribution into the parents' 529 account (assuming that particular 529 plan accepts contributions from a non-owner). Another easy way to "gift" a 529 plan contribution into an account for a grandchild is to make the check out in the name of the 529 plan and hand the check to the parent who can make sure it is contributed on behalf of the grandchild. For gift tax purposes, the grandparent is still the one making the contribution and can make the five-year election discussed previously in this guide.

Invite friends and family to help. Spread the message that you have opened a 529 college savings account for your child and that you would prefer that birthday and holiday gifts be directed into your account rather than be spent on a store-bought items. These contributions can add up to a considerable amount over time. GradSave.com is a website that makes this process easy.

Consider professional assistance. We suggest you consult with experienced and knowledgeable financial, tax, and/ or legal advisors about all the matters discussed in this book. The issues are complex. Be aware that for some financial advisors, 529 plans and ESAs are a new phenomenon. If you are working with one, ask which particular 529 plans are available through the advisor and what makes one 529 plan better than another. In interviewing prospective advisors you might even ask whether they have opened their own 529 accounts. It helps to know that the professional you are relying on has personal experience with 529 plans.

Be flexible with your college planning. Programs and investments will continue to evolve. Tax laws will change and so will your own circumstances. Review your financial situation periodically and make adjustments whenever it seems appropriate.

EMPLOYER-SPONSORED 529 PLANS

You may discover that your employer is offering a special group enrollment process for 529 plans. This can be an easy way to open an account and make contributions, but you should understand that an employer-sponsored 529 plan is handled on an after-tax basis and there are no additional federal income or payroll tax savings.

However, there may be other advantages that make the employer's choice of 529 plans valuable to you. Before contributing, find out whether there are special cost reductions or waivers or resources such as college planning workshops or limited-access Web sites.

Just be sure to recognize that the 529 plan(s) selected by your employer may not be best option for you, and that you can always open accounts on your own in other 529 plans.

COLLEGE SAVINGS ALTERNATIVES

How They Compare

Year 2014 Rules	529 Plan	Coverdell Education Savings Account	Qualifying U.S. Savings Bonds
Federal Income Tax	Non-deductible contributions; withdrawn earnings excluded from income to extent of qualified higher education expenses	Same as 529 plan except earnings withdrawn for qualified K-12 expenses also excluded	Tax-deferred for federal; tax-free for state; certain post-1989 EE and I bonds may be redeemed federal tax-free for qualified higher education expenses
Federal Gift Tax Treatment	Contributions treated as completed gifts; apply $14,000 annual exclusion, or up to $70,000 with 5-year election	Same as 529 plan but 5-year election available only under special circumstances	No gift as qualifying bonds must be owned by the parent
Federal Estate Tax Treatment	Value removed from donor's gross estate; partial inclusion for death during a 5-year election period	Value removed from donor's gross estate	Value included in bond owner's gross estate
Maximum Investment	Established by the program; many in excess of $300,000 per beneficiary	$2,000 per beneficiary per year combined from all sources	$10,000 face value per year, per owner, per type of bond through electronic purchase
Qualified Expenses	Tuition, fees, books, supplies, equipment, and special needs; room and board for minimum half-time students	Same as 529 plan plus additional categories of K-12 expenses	Tuition and fees
Able to Change Beneficiary?	Yes, to another member of the beneficiary's family	Yes, to another member of the beneficiary's family	Not applicable
Time/Age Restrictions	None unless imposed by the program	Contributions stop when beneficiary reaches age 18; use account by age 30	Bond purchaser must be at least 24 years old at time of bond issue
Income Restriction	None	Ability to contribute phases out for incomes between $190,000 and $220,000 (joint filers) or $95,000 and $110,000 (single)	Interest exclusion phases out for incomes between $113,950 and $143,950 (joint filers) or $76,000 and $91,000 (single)
Federal Financial Aid	Counted as asset of parent if owner is parent or dependent student	Counted as asset of parent if owner is parent or dependent student	Counted as asset of bond owner
Investments	Menu of investment strategies as developed by the program	Broad range of securities and certain other investments	Interest-earning bond backed by full faith and credit of U.S. government
Use for Nonqualifying Expenses	Withdrawn earnings subject to federal tax and 10% penalty	Withdrawn earnings subject to federal tax and 10% penalty	No penalty; interest on redeemed bonds included in federal income

Roth IRA	Traditional IRA	UGMA/UTMA	Mutual Funds
Non-deductible contributions; withdraw tax-free if certain requirements are met; no early withdrawal penalty if used for qualified higher education expenses	Deductible or non-deductible contributions; withdrawals in excess of basis subject to tax; no early withdrawal penalty if used for qualified higher education expenses	Earnings and gains taxed to minor; first $1,000 of unearned income is tax exempt; unearned income over $2,000 for certain children through age 23 is taxed at parents' rate	Earnings and gains taxed in year realized; special lower tax rates for certain dividends and capital gains
No gift involved	No gift involved	Transfers treated as completed gift; apply $14,000 annual gift exclusion	No gift involved; direct payments of tuition not considered gifts
Value included in the owner's gross estate	Value included in the owner's gross estate	Value removed from donor's gross estate unless donor remains as custodian	Value included in the owner's gross estate
$5,500 ($6,500 for taxpayers age 50 and over)	$5,500 ($6,500 for taxpayers age 50 and over)	No limit	No limit
Same as 529 plan	Same as 529 plan	No restrictions	No restrictions
Not applicable	Not applicable	No; represents an irrevocable gift to the child	Not applicable
Withdraw earnings tax-free only after five years and age 59½	Withdraw without penalty only after age 59½	Custodianship terminates when minor reaches age established under state law (generally 18 or 21)	None
Must have taxable compensation; contribution limit phases out for incomes between $181,000 and $191,000 (joint) or $114,000 and $129,000 (single)	Must have taxable compensation; amount deductible reduced or eliminated for taxpayers who participate in an employer retirement plan and have income above certain limits	None	None
Not counted as asset; withdrawals of principal and interest counted as financial aid income	Not counted as asset; withdrawals of principal and interest counted as financial aid income	Counted as student's asset	Counted as asset of the owner
Broad range of securities and certain other investments	Broad range of securities and certain other investments	As permitted under state laws	Mutual funds
Taxable portion of withdrawal prior to age 59½ also subject to 10% early withdrawal penalty	Taxable portion of withdrawal prior to age 59½ also subject to 10% early withdrawal penalty	Funds must be used for benefit of the minor	No restrictions